E-Textiles

CHERRY LAKE PUBLISHING • ANN ARBOR, MICHIGAN

by Jan Toth-Chernin

A Note to Adults: Please review the instructions for the activities in this book before allowing children to do them. Be sure to help them with any activities you do not think they can safely complete on their own.

A Note to Kids: Be sure to ask an adult for help with these activities when you need it. Always put your safety first!

Published in the United States of America by Cherry Lake Publishing
Ann Arbor, Michigan
www.cherrylakepublishing.com

Series Editor: Kristin Fontichiaro
Photo Credits: Cover and pages 1, 12, 22, and 23, ©Bekathwia/
www.flickr.com/CC-BY-SA-2.0; page 5, ©Schmarty/www.flickr.com/
CC-BY-2.0; page 13, ©s p e x/www.flickr.com/CC-BY-SA-2.0; page 15,
©The U.S. Army/www.flickr.com/CC-BY-2.0; page 17, ©carterse/
www.flickr.com/CC-BY-SA-2.0; page 18, ©lovstromp/www.flickr.com/
CC-BY-2.0; page 24, ©dam/www.flickr.com/CC-BY-2.0; page 27,
©mjtmail (tiggy)/www.flickr.com / CC-BY-2.0

Library of Congress Cataloging-in-Publication Data
Toth-Chernin, Jan.
  E-textiles/by Jan Toth-Chernin.
     pages cm.—(Makers as innovators) (Innovation library)
  Summary: "Learn about the exciting new technology behind e-textiles and find
out how to create e-textile projects of your own" — Provided by publisher.
  Audience: 4 to 6.
  Includes bibliographical references and index.
  ISBN 978-1-62431-140-6 (lib. bdg.)—ISBN 978-1-62431-206-9 (e-book)—
ISBN 978-1-62431-272-4 (pbk.)
  1. Textile fabrics—Technological innovations—Juvenile literature. 2. Textile
industry—Technological innovations—Juvenile literature. 3. New products—
Juvenile literature. I. Title.
  TS1775.T68 2013
  677.6—dc23   2013006656

Cherry Lake Publishing would like to acknowledge the work of The Partnership for
21st Century Skills. Please visit www.p21.org for more information.

Printed in the United States of America
Corporate Graphics Inc.
July 2013
CLFA13

Contents

Chapter 1   **What Are E-Textiles?**   4

Chapter 2   **Sewing with Electronics**   9

Chapter 3   **Beginning Projects with Soft Circuits**   19

Chapter 4   **Microcontrollers**   23

Chapter 5   **Light It Up!**   26

Glossary   30

Find Out More   31

Index   32

About the Author   32

Chapter 1

What Are E-Textiles?

Can you imagine making a phone call from your T-shirt? Would you like to have a scarf that gets tighter as the wind kicks up? These are not quite reality yet, but fashion designers, artists, and scientists are working together to combine **textiles** and technology. The future of your clothing could be electronic.

E-textile is short for electronic or electro-textile. E-textiles are also called **conductive** clothing, electronic clothing, and soft **circuits**. Electronics, small computers, or other digital devices are built into in them. Special conductive thread or paints can be sewn or applied to the fabric as well.

Smart fabrics do not only sense the environment but also react to it. One example might be a shirt that warms you when it's cold outside, cleans itself when it's dirty, lights up when it gets dark, or protects the wearer from a fall. Smart clothes could monitor your workout and give you advice on how to train. A shirt with a pocket that charges mobile phones would be

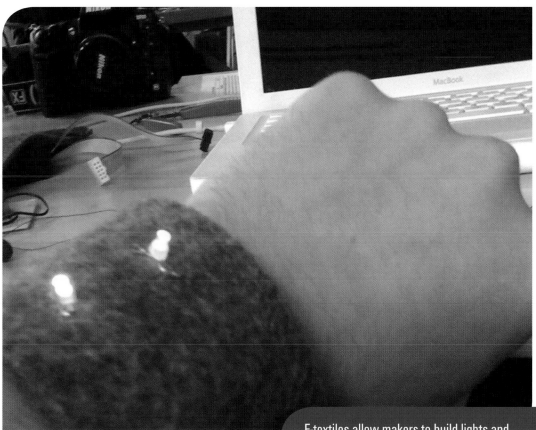

E-textiles allow makers to build lights and other electronic devices into clothes and other wearable accessories, such as this cuff.

convenient. Smart fabrics are part of a larger category called digital wearables. The field of building advanced technology into textile fibers is sometimes called fibertronics.

Smart clothes and e-textiles can act like a second skin to help monitor what goes on under real skin. Electronic or digital **sensors** woven into or painted onto the clothes can track people's body changes and surrounding environmental conditions. Some research-ers are hopeful that they will be able to use the body's natural energy to power smart clothes. Because the sensors are part of the clothing, they can be placed in direct contact with a person's skin and can detect an amazing range of information about the wearer.

Sharing the information gathered from these clothes has the potential to change the way online communities work. Athletes might compare their data with that of their friends or professional athletes. Information during sporting events could be shared with viewers as it happens. Video games could get more personal.

What happens when fabric becomes programmable? Furniture manufacturers in Sweden are interested in fabrics that can change pattern and color. This could help people who can't make up their minds about which sofa they want. Researchers are also experimenting with furniture that can heat up. This would help people who live in cold places save energy because they could run their furnaces less in the winter. The E-Textile Laboratory at Virginia Tech University in Blacksburg, Virginia, is embedding electronics into rugs. The rug lights up as people move across it. This has the potential to help track people in low-visibility situations. It could also help guide traffic during evacuations in large buildings.

E-textiles and smart fabrics are becoming important for improving health and safety. Shirts that relieve back pain and remind patients to take their medications might soon become common. Boaters are testing life jackets that have sensors to help rescuers find them. Cyclists are wearing shirts with turn signals and lights built in to prevent traffic accidents. Firefighters may eventually enter a burning building in uniforms that collect information and map directions for safe return routes. Each year almost 50,000 Americans become disabled because of swelling associated with the disease diabetes. Socks with conductive threads and pressure sensors could monitor and prevent swelling to avoid this.

Medical data gathered from these wearables can also be shared online with health care providers. This could allow patients to leave hospitals early and still be carefully monitored by their doctors.

The fashion industry is equally excited about wearable electronics. While one-of-a-kind designs have often sported electronic accessories, designers are now producing electronic clothing that is within the budget of many Americans. Conductive thread, flexible wire, lights, and computers are frequently being built into T-shirts, gloves, and other wearables.

What smart item would you most like to have hanging in your closet? By learning a few sewing techniques and understanding a few basic principles of electricity, you could produce some unique wearables. The following chapters can help you get started working on your own projects that combine technology and fashion.

High-Low Tech Research

Professor Leah Buechley directs the High-Low Tech research group at the Massachusetts Institute of Technology Media Lab in Cambridge, Massachusetts. Her group combines high-tech materials such as electronics, computers, and conductive materials with low-tech resources like thread, paper, paints, and fabrics. Buechley's team believes that the future of technology is to inspire individuals to hack, design, and build their own products. This intersection of crafting, manufacturing, and computers brings technology into everyday objects. It could affect society in countless ways.

Chapter 2

Sewing with Electronics

When assembling electronic circuits on fabrics, it helps to have a sewing machine. It is not necessary, however. The projects in this book can be created without one. A lot of tools and techniques are the same for hand sewing and machine sewing. If you have a machine, go ahead and use it. It's a lot faster than sewing by hand.

Sewing Supplies

Here are a few supplies you will need to work on your own e-textile projects:

- Embroidery hoop: This keeps your fabric pulled tight as you work.
- Fabric scissors: These are long scissors with extra-sharp metal blades. Don't cut paper with them because that will make them dull.
- Needle threader: Conductive thread frays easily. Using one of these will help.

- Notions: These are buttons, sequins, snaps, and fabric for decorating your projects.
- Polyester thread: This is stronger than cotton thread and won't shrink when you wash it. Embroidery thread for decorative stitches is also handy.
- Seam ripper: This is used to rip out mistakes in your sewing. It is also helpful for taking apart clothing to use in new projects.
- Sewing needle: These come in different sizes. A number 7 needle is best for sewing with conductive thread.
- Straight pins: These hold layers of materials together. Thin ones work best.

Stitches to Learn

There are four different stitches to master for hand sewing your projects: a running stitch, a whipstitch, a topstitch, and a backstitch.

Running stitch. This stitch is used to sew two pieces of fabric together and to create a circuit with conductive thread. Tie a knot at the end of your thread. Hold the two layers of fabric together. Push your needle up through both layers and pull gently until the knot stops you from pulling any farther. Now point the sharp end of your needle downward, piercing the fabric about $\frac{1}{8}$ inch (3 millimeters) away. Repeat again and again. Don't tug too hard, or the fabric will pucker and wrinkle. When you become more experienced, you'll be able to move your needle up and down, above and below the fabric several times before pulling the thread through. This creates stitches about $\frac{1}{8}$ to $\frac{1}{4}$ inch (3 to 6 mm) apart.

Whipstitch. This basic stitch wraps around the edges of fabric to keep it from unraveling. Start on the underside of the fabric. Push the needle to the top near the edge of the fabric. Wrap the thread around the edge of the fabric and push the needle up from underneath again. Continue until you reach the end.

Different e-textile projects will require different kinds of stitching.

Topstitch. This is a running stitch to sew one fabric on top of another (like a patch). Push the needle from under the bottom fabric through to the top fabric. Use short running stitches to keep the fabrics together.

Backstitch. Instead of tying a knot when you are finishing stitching, try a backstitch to secure the

These jeans set off an alarm when the wearer has been sitting too long, encouraging him or her to stand up and stretch.

stitches. Just stitch backwards three or four times. This will be important when sewing complete circuits.

Tips and Tricks

A few tricks can help make projects go more smoothly. Pinning layers of fabric together will keep them in place and allow better stitching. Lay the fabric out on a smooth, hard surface. If using pattern pieces from paper, place them on the fabric. Try to put the patterns near one another so you don't waste fabric. Pin the pieces so they stay in place while you cut. If a pattern says "fold," line that edge up with the fold in the fabric.

Ironed seams make a garment look well made. If the seams are bunched and uneven, people might get a bad first impression of the sewing project. After you finish sewing a seam, iron the seam before attaching another piece of fabric. This will keep the project crisp and professional looking.

Some projects require you to sew circles or tight curves. Use fabric scissors to snip the seam so that the fabric will hold the correct shape when it is turned right-side out. This gets rid of extra fabric.

Sewing isn't just for girls! In this photo, a U.S. Army soldier serving in Iraq mends his uniform on a sewing machine.

Electronic Supplies

In addition to sewing supplies, you will need a variety of electronic devices to complete your e-textile projects:

- Alligator clips: These are wires with clips. They will help test to see if circuits are working.
- Batteries: In this book, all of the projects will use coin cell batteries (CR2032). They are small but powerful enough to light up an **LED.** You can find these batteries at drugstores and

hardware stores. All batteries have a positive and negative side. Electricity flows from the positive to the negative side. When assembling your creations, it's important to make sure that the electricity flows from the correct lead of the battery to the correct side of the LED.

- Battery holder: Like batteries themselves, there are many types of battery holders. The BS7 is easy to sew. It can be found in hobby stores or purchased online.

- Conductive thread: Like wire, this thread allows electricity to flow through it. It usually has metal built into its fiber. It can be purchased online.

- Electrical tape: This tape is used to wrap wires and connections.

- LED. This is an electronic mini-lightbulb. Electricity flows through an LED in only one direction. It's important to remember that the positive side of the circuit must be connected to an LED's long lead (or leg) and the negative side of the circuit must be connected to the short lead.

LED lights come in a wide variety of colors.

- Multimeter: This device measures power and much more. It is available at hardware stores.
- Needle-nose pliers: These long, narrow gripping tools are used to bend leads and wires.
- Pliers. These tools are handy when gripping and holding small objects. They can also be used to bend and strip wires.

Sewing E-Textiles with a Sewing Machine

Many people prefer to use a sewing machine instead of sewing by hand when creating garments and home decorations. Your sewing machine will work fine for the parts of your project that you would stitch with regular thread. However, conductive thread may not be compatible with all sewing machines. Sewing machines draw thread from two places: a spool that feeds from the top of the machine down to the needle and a special spool called a bobbin that unspools from beneath the needle. The two threads link together to create a stitch. Some sewing machines can use special thread, like conductive thread, in one spool but not in the other spool. Check your machine's owner's manual and make a sample before working on your actual project!

Chapter 3

Beginning Projects with Soft Circuits

D o you think that you have an electric personality? We all do! The human body is conductive and stores electricity. Most touch screens work by interacting with this electricity. Regular gloves prevent this interaction from happening. Using conductive thread on the fingers of the glove solves that problem, letting you keep your hands warm while using a touch screen.

Make a Gadget Glove

Here's how to make gloves you can use with a touch screen:

1. Put on a pair of gloves and try to use your touch screen. Mark the spots on the tip of the index finger and thumb where your glove touches the screen.

2. Sew a ¼ inch by ¼ inch (6 mm by 6 mm) square on the marks using conductive thread. Sew a set of running stitches in one direction. Then sew a second set of stitches that crosses over the top of the first set. Do this on both gloves.

3. If your gloves don't work properly, try adding more conductive thread to the inside of the glove fingers.

Tips for Working with Conductive Thread

- Threading a needle with conductive thread is tricky. The thread tends to fray. Run the thread through beeswax to help keep the threads together.
- Keep your stitches close together to make the circuit strong.
- Put a dab of hot glue or fabric paint on knots or any other loose threads to secure them.

Experiment with Switches

A switch is a device that opens and closes an electrical circuit. Devices such as metal snaps, hooks, and zippers can all be used as switches in soft circuit projects.

To turn a zipper into a switch, the upper or lower teeth opposite from each other can be sewn with conductive thread. The path from each zipper tooth can be continued to complete the circuit. When the zipper closes, the teeth connect and close the circuit.

Grommets are great switches when creating wearables or accessories using a drawstring. Make a pouch and sew a strip of conductive fabric onto grommets along the top. Then add a few LEDs and close the pouch with a drawstring. You'll have a cool shopping bag that lights up.

Soft or pressure-sensitive switches come in handy when working with objects like stuffed animals or T-shirts. These allow the wearer to control the operation of the circuit manually. To make one, all that's needed are two layers of conductive fabric and a thin middle layer of regular fabric. Netted fabric works well between the two conductive layers. When pressure is applied to the top layer, the circuit is closed.

A zipper switch activates as the part of the zipper with conductive thread is closed.

Chapter 4

Microcontrollers

Microcontrollers are like miniature computers. They are found in all sorts of everyday objects, from microwaves to remote controls. A microcontroller acts as the "brain" of a circuit. The Arduino is an open-source microcontroller. Open

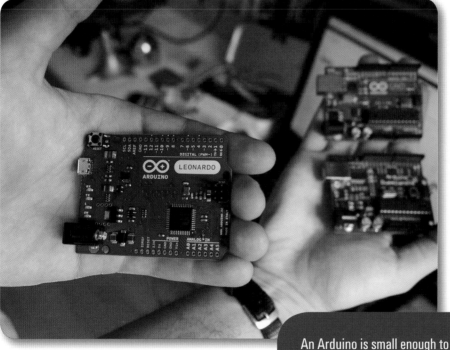

An Arduino is small enough to fit in the palm of your hand.

source means it can be modified and shared for free with anyone. The Arduino attracted the attention of Leah Buechley, a professor at the Massachusetts Institute of Technology (MIT) in Cambridge,

Open-Source Technology

Many people who tinker with e-textiles are interested in open-source technology. What does it mean for something to be open source? It means that the creators of an invention share their blueprints and designs with anyone else who wants to see, use, change, or adapt them. The inventors of the Arduino microcontroller made their plans open source, making it easier for Leah Buechley to adapt them. In turn, her plans for the LilyPad are also open source. Open source can move innovation faster and create a culture of shared creations.

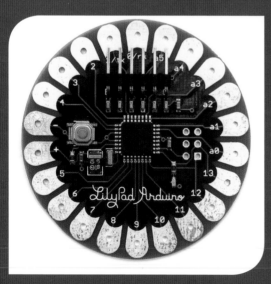

Massachusetts. Buechley used the Arduino as the basis of a microcontroller called the LilyPad. The Lilypad is a small microcontroller designed to work with e-textiles and other digital wearables. It can be sewn with conductive thread onto fabrics and can be programmed to control a variety of electronic devices. A LilyPad (shown on the cover of this book) can control the behavior of connected LED lights. It can cause them to blink, fade, twinkle, or pulse.

Limor Fried, a former electronics designer from MIT, has developed another sewable board called Flora. Like the LilyPad, it is circular. However, Flora is ¼ inch smaller than the LilyPad. Size is an important thing to consider when creating digital wearables. Flora also has a **USB** connection. That means it is easier to update and program than the LilyPad. In addition, Flora's USB connection allows it to connect to a keyboard, mouse, or cell phone. Plans are in the works to release Gemma, a microcontroller similar to Flora that is only 1 inch (2.54 centimeters) wide!

Chapter 5

Light It Up!

There are many ways to transform ordinary objects into glowing, eye-catching wearables. Conductive ink, electroluminescent (EL) wire, and conductive fabric are great options to use for easy projects that shine.

EL wire is thin copper wire coated with a substance that glows when electricity is applied to it. Backpacks, skirts, shoes, and dog collars are all easy projects to tackle using this colorful wire.

Fashion Fly

You can add flair to a skirt by attaching EL wire to light up the town. Here's how:

1. Select a light-colored or light-patterned skirt in a midweight fabric. The light coloring will allow the light from the wire to be visible. A skirt with a zipper in the back works best. The skirt should also have a lining.

2. You need a pocket inside your skirt, between the lining and the outside fabric, where you can stash the switch that will turn the wire on and off. Cut out a pocket shape that is ½ inch (13 mm) larger on all sides than the switch on your EL wire. Sew the

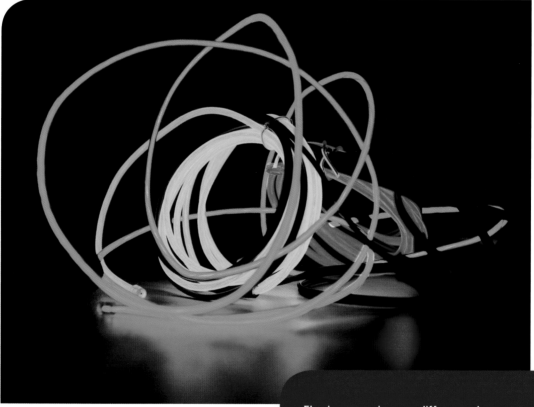

EL wire comes in many different colors.

pocket on the inside of the skirt next to the zipper. Sew only three of the sides so that the switch can be taken in and out of the skirt.

3. Place the switch into the pocket and let the wire hang out on the right side of the skirt. Tape the wire down.

4. Trace the outline of the wire onto your skirt with sewing chalk. Allow $\frac{1}{8}$ inch (3 mm) on each side of the wire to create a tube for the wire.

5. With regular thread, sew along these lines from the outside of the skirt and through the lining to create a tunnel for the wire. You can do this by hand using a backstitch. It will be faster if you use a sewing machine.

6. Cut a small hole at the top of the skirt near the switch and insert the EL wire. Watch out for bunching!

7. Sew the top and bottom of the tube closed with regular thread.

Go someplace fun! Most switches on EL wire are programmed so users can select how they want their wire to glow: steady, blinking, or off and on.

Conductive Ink and Paints

Ink has been around for ages. Now it's being used to print circuits, sensors, and switches directly onto fabric and paper. For example, sleeping bags printed with conductive inks help keep campers' feet warm. You can experiment with conductive ink and paint for yourself. There are paints on the market that are photochromic, which means that they can change color when exposed to sunlight. Try decorating a backpack for a soft, safe glow.

Bare Conductive, a company in England, has created a conductive ink pen that can be used on paper, fabric, plastics, and wood. Soon conductive body paint will be on the market. Making creative costumes just got easier!

Glossary

circuits (SIR-kits) complete paths for electrical current

conductive (kuhn-DUK-tiv) capable of allowing electricity to pass through

grommets (GRAH-mits) metal or plastic rings that can be sewn into fabric

LED (ELL-EE-DEE) a small light that can be switched on or off; LED stands for light emitting diode

sensors (SEN-sorz) instruments that can detect and measure changes and transmit the information to a controlling device

textiles (TEK-stylz) woven or knitted fabrics or cloths

USB (YOO ESS BEE) a standard type of cable and port that is commonly used to connect computers and other electronic devices; USB stands for Universal Serial Bus

Find Out More

BOOKS

Eng, Diana. *Fashion Geek: Clothing, Accessories, Tech.* Cincinnati, OH: North Light Books, 2009.

Lewis, Alison, and Fang-Yu Lin. *Switch Craft: Battery-Powered Crafts to Make and Sew.* New York: Potter Craft, 2008.

WEB SITES

Instructables
www.instructables.com
Find instructions for a variety of fun e-textile projects.

LilyPond
http://lilypond.media.mit.edu
Check out some e-textile projects others have created.

Index

Arduino microcontroller, 23–25

batteries, 15–16
Buechley, Leah, 8, 24–25

circuits, 21–22
conductive thread, 7, 8, 9, 10, 11,
    16, 18, 19, 20, 21, 25, 28

electricity, 8, 16, 19, 26
electroluminescent (EL) wire, 26–29

Fashion Fly project, 26–29

Gadget Gloves project, 19–20

knots, 11, 12, 20

LEDs, 15, 16, 17, 21, 25
LilyPad microcontroller, 24, 25

Massachusetts Institute of
    Technology (MIT), 8, 24–25
microcontrollers, 23–25

needles, 9, 10, 11, 12, 18, 20

paints, 4, 5, 8, 20, 29

seams, 10, 14
sensors, 5–6, 7, 29
sewing machines, 9, 18, 28
stitches, 10–12, 14, 18, 20, 28
supplies, 9–10, 15–17
switches, 21–22, 27, 28, 29

zippers, 21, 26, 28

About the Author

Jan Toth-Chernin is the director of information and technology at Greenhills School in Ann Arbor, Michigan. She has enjoyed tinkering for as long as she can remember.